Wonderful Winter

by Jennifer Marino Walters • illustrated by John Nez

Rocking Chair Kids™
AN IMPRINT OF RED CHAIR PRESS
Egremont, MA

Rocking Chair Kids™ books are published by Red Chair Press.

Red Chair Press LLC   PO Box 333   South Egremont, MA 01258

www.redchairpress.com

About the Author

Jennifer Marino Walters is a writer and editor specializing in family and parenting topics. She has written for major media such as *Los Angeles Times, Reader's Digest, Parenting, Scholastic News,* and Care.com. Jennifer lives with her husband, twin boys and daughter in the Washington D.C. area.

About the Artist

John Nez has illustrated books of all sorts…and he's written a few books as well. John sometimes works in traditional mediums with real paints. He also makes digital art on his computer. John lives in Seattle where he enjoys the natural wonders of the Northwest.

Publisher's Cataloging-In-Publication Data

Walters, Jennifer Marino.
  Wonderful winter / by Jennifer Marino Walters ; illustrated by John Nez.

     pages : illustrations ; cm.

  Summary: "Winter can be quite wonderful with soft white snow. It's a season for bundling up in warm clothes and making new friends. What else does winter mean to you?"--Provided by publisher.

  Includes the concepts of sequence, counting, letter recognition, and up/down.

  ISBN: 978-1-63440-046-6 (library hardcover)
  ISBN: 978-1-63440-121-0 (paperback)
  ISBN: 978-1-63440-125-8 (ebook)

  1. Winter--Juvenile fiction. 2. Nature--Juvenile fiction. 3. Counting--Juvenile fiction. 4. Order--Juvenile fiction. 5. Alphabet--Juvenile fiction. 6. Winter--Fiction. 7. Nature--Fiction. 8. Counting--Fiction. 9. Alphabet--Fiction. 10. Picture books. I. Nez, John A. II. Title.

PZ7.1.W358 Wo 2016

[E]   2015958037

Printed in the United States of America
Distributed in the U.S. by Lerner Publisher Services. www.lernerbooks.com

0516 1 LPSF16

Winter has arrived. Brrr. It's cold outside!

It's time to bundle up.
Put on a coat and pull up the zipper.

Ah... nice and warm! But what are we forgetting?

That's right — a hat, a scarf, mittens, and boots.

Now we are ready to go outside. Open the door.

It's snowing!

Touch the falling snowflakes.
How many can you count?

Let's build a snowman.
Give him eyes, a nose,
a mouth, and two arms.

All done! Wave hello to the snowman!

Now we'll go sledding.
Pull your sled
up the hill.

Ready? Sit down and hold on tight.

Wheeee!

That was fast!

Let's make snow angels.
Don't forget to move your arms and legs.

Those are great angels! Blow each one a kiss.

Now let's go ice skating.
Slide your finger around the ice.

Whoa! That's slippery!

All that fun has made us hungry. What's for dinner?

Yum! Alphabet soup!

What letters do you see?
What word can you spell?

And now some hot cocoa for dessert.
Tap the white marshmallows.

Let's drink it by the warm fire. Nice and cozy!
We can dream about all our winter fun...

...and wait for spring to arrive!